INSIDE THE MINDS OF SEX TRAFFICKING VICTIMS

INSIDE THE MINDS OF SEX TRAFFICKING VICTIMS

Training Manual for Law Enforcement, Counselors, Medical Professionals, Military, Nonprofits, and Service Providers

SULA LAEL

CONTENTS

PART ONE: SEX TRAFFICKING

PART TWO: SATANIC RITUAL ABUSE / OCCULT TRAFFICKING

INTRODUCTION

Welcome

I'm deeply honored that you've picked up this book. Whether you're in law enforcement, social work, the medical or mental health field, the hospitality or travel industry, a nonprofit leader, safe home staff, or simply someone moved by compassion—thank you. Your willingness to grow in understanding the realities of sex trafficking and to walk with survivors in their healing journey is both rare and urgently needed.

This book was born from two deeply intertwined sources: my own lived experience as a survivor of sex trafficking and ritual abuse, and over a decade of working across the continuum of care in the anti-trafficking movement. In 2022, I founded Take Flight Survivors, a 501(c)(3) nonprofit committed to embracing survivors with support, encouragement, and comprehensive care as they transition from exploitation into safety, freedom, and restoration.

I didn't write this book to simply inform you—I wrote it to equip you. I hope that it helps you respond from a place that is trauma-informed, survivor-informed, and rooted in deep compassion and insight.

While many anti-trafficking resources stop at awareness or surface-level training, *Inside the Minds of Sex Trafficking Survivors* goes further. This book gently guides you into some of the deeper, often hidden dynamics that survivors live with daily—things like complex trauma, dissociation, mind control programming, ritual abuse, and organized exploitation. These are difficult realities, but they are not rare. I've lived them, and I've walked closely with others who have too. This book gives language to what many survivors have not yet been able to speak.

If you're ready to go even deeper, this book also serves as a companion to the online course *Working with Sex Trafficking Survivors*, available through Take Flight Academy. The course expands on these topics with practical tools and strategies to help you respond effectively—whether your role is in housing, counseling, advocacy, crisis intervention, case management, or survivor support.

You can access the course here:
www.TakeFlightSurvivors.org/Academy

At Take Flight Survivors, we believe that the journey from trauma to transformation must be surrounded by empathy, clarity, and evidence-informed tools. We train service providers in trauma-informed care that honors the voice and agency of survivors, while equipping them with tools for long-term healing and reintegration. No two healing journeys are the same—and there are no one-size-fits-all answers.

It's important to remember this: imposing belief systems or worldviews on someone who isn't ready can cause harm. Survivors need safe, supportive environments where their autonomy is respected and their healing journey is honored—without pressure, assumptions, or control. True healing is cultivated through trust, safety, choice, and consistent care.

I hope that every survivor would come to recognize their worth, reclaim their voice, and rise in their identity as whole, empowered individuals—free from the labels and limitations placed on them by trauma and exploitation.

By the time you finish this book, I hope you'll be better equipped to recognize trafficking situations, respond wisely, and support survivors with compassion, dignity, and skill. You are stepping into vital work—and I'm truly grateful you've chosen to engage.

With honor and gratitude,
Sula Lael
Founder, Take Flight Survivors
TakeFlightSurvivors.org
SulaLael.com

NOTE FOR CHRISTIAN READERS

If you are a follower of Jesus and seeking a faith-based perspective on survivor care, a companion version of this book is available. It includes additional biblical insights, spiritual applications, and prayer-based guidance for supporting survivors. Check out *Faith-Based Inside the Minds of Sex Trafficking Victims* available at SulaLael.com/Books.

PART ONE: SEX TRAFFICKING

CHAPTER 1

WHAT IS SEX TRAFFICKING?

Sex trafficking is a form of modern-day slavery where individuals are forced, coerced, or deceived into the commercial sex trade against their will. It includes any child involved in commercial sex. Sex traffickers often target vulnerable individuals with a history of abuse and use violence, threats, lies, false promises, debt bondage, or other forms of control and manipulation to keep victims involved in the sex industry.

Professionals and service providers need to understand the various types of sex trafficking in the United States and become familiar with the facts and statistics surrounding this issue. This knowledge is critical to identifying victims, preventing exploitation, and providing informed, effective support.

TYPES OF SEX TRAFFICKING IN AMERICA

Sex trafficking can take many forms. Below are some of the most commonly identified:

1. Intimate partner trafficking – The trafficker is a romantic partner or spouse.
2. Familial trafficking – The trafficker is a family member.
3. Illicit massage business trafficking – The trafficker runs a front business, such as a massage parlor, to conceal the commercial sex trade.
4. Child sexual abuse material (CSAM) trafficking – Children are exploited to produce and distribute explicit content for profit, either in organized rings or by individuals.
5. Pornography trafficking – Individuals are forced or coerced into performing in pornography against their will.
6. Occult crime / ritual abuse trafficking – Victims are subjected to ritual abuse in combination with sexual exploitation. These crimes often involve organized, multi-perpetrator abuse.
7. Strip club / cantina trafficking – Individuals are forced to work in establishments like strip clubs or cantinas and are exploited through commercial sex acts.
8. Online exploitation and cybersex trafficking – Traffickers exploit victims using livestreams, webcams, or digital platforms, often involving coercion or sale of explicit content.
9. Survival sex trafficking – Individuals, especially youth or those experiencing homelessness, are

manipulated into exchanging sex for basic needs like food, shelter, protection, or transportation.

10. Gang-controlled trafficking – Victims are trafficked as part of a gang's criminal enterprise, often involving threats, violence, and coercion.

11. Escort service trafficking – Traffickers pose as legitimate escort agencies but force individuals into commercial sex under the guise of legal work.

FACTS AND STATISTICS

It is challenging to find accurate statistics and facts about sex trafficking, as it is underreported. However, it is important to understand the scope of the issue. Some statistics and facts include:

- The United States is one of the top three countries in which trafficking originates. (U.S. Department of State, Trafficking in Persons Report)
- The top three states where sex trafficking is reported: California, Texas, and Florida. (Polaris)
- 50–90% of child sex trafficking victims have been involved in the child welfare system. (Child Welfare Information Gateway)
- The U.S. is both a source and destination for sex trafficking involving men, women, transgender individuals, and children. (U.S. Department of State)
- A child is being groomed for exploitation every two minutes. (UNICEF)

- Girls as young as 5–6 years old in the U.S. have been exploited for profit by traffickers. (U.S. Department of Justice)
- Children may be born into trafficking or coerced from toddler age—especially in familial trafficking cases. (THORN.org)
- Average entry age into the sex trade is 12–14 years for girls, and 11–13 years for boys. (National Center for Missing and Exploited Children)
- An estimated 4.5 million people are trafficked annually for forced labor through sexual exploitation. (International Labour Organization)
- As many as 100,000–300,000 American children are at risk of sex trafficking each year. (U.S. Department of Justice)
- Research across nine countries found 60–75% of prostituted women were raped, 70–95% were physically assaulted, and 68% met PTSD criteria similar to combat veterans. (Farley, Melissa et al., 2003)
- 70% of female trafficking victims are trafficked into commercial sex, including pornography and stripping. (U.S. Department of Justice)
- Up to 95% of victims have a history of childhood sexual abuse. (Melissa Farley, Psychiatric Times)
- 89% of women in prostitution expressed a desire to escape but lacked survival alternatives. (Journal of Trauma Practice)
- In 2025, the U.S. Department of Health and Human Services reported over 291,000 unaccompanied minors were released into the U.S.

without tracking, with 32,000 failing to appear in court. Some were released to traffickers.

- 1 in 7 children reported missing to the National Center for Missing and Exploited Children became victims of trafficking—88% of them had prior involvement in foster care. (Polaris)

GLOSSARY OF TRAFFICKING AND PIMP CULTURE TERMS

1. 403 / Four-Oh-Three – A code word used to refer to a "hoe" or prostituted person. Some pimps use numerical slang to mask conversations from outsiders.
2. Bottom (or Bottom B*) – The trafficker's most trusted girl, usually a victim who helps manage or recruit other girls, enforces rules, and collects money. She is still being exploited, but may be perceived to have "status."
3. Stable – The group of prostituted individuals or trafficking victims under the control of a single pimp or trafficker.
4. Quota – The amount of money a victim is expected to earn in a day or night. If they don't meet it, consequences like violence, withholding food, or emotional manipulation and abuse may follow.
5. Turn Out – The process of initiating someone into prostitution or trafficking. A pimp may refer to "turning someone out" as a way of breaking them in.

6. Choose Up – A victim is said to "choose up" when she leaves one pimp for another, often under pressure or manipulation. This is falsely presented as a "choice" but is often coerced or forced.

7. Reckless Eyeballing – A street term used when someone makes eye contact with another pimp's girl or a victim makes eye contact with another pimp. This is seen as disrespectful and could result in violence.

8. Gorilla Pimp – A trafficker who uses physical violence and intimidation to control victims. Known for brutality, as opposed to a "Romeo pimp" who uses charm and false love.

9. Romeo Pimp / Loverboy – A trafficker who uses emotional manipulation, romance, or false promises of love to lure and control victims. This involves love bombing, gaslighting, coercion, and manipulation.

10. Wifey / Wife-in-Law – Other girls, working for the same pimp. Victims may refer to one another this way, especially if they are trafficked as part of a stable.

11. Out of Pocket – A victim is said to be "out of pocket" when she is disobeying her pimp, working independently, or talking to another trafficker.

12. Circuit – A series of cities or locations where trafficked individuals are taken to be sold. Common circuits exist across the U.S. and are rotated to avoid detection.

13. Family / Folks – Slang used within pimp culture to refer to the trafficker and their victims, often in a distorted "family" dynamic that reinforces loyalty and control.
14. Choosing Fee / Choose Fee – Money a new pimp pays to take control of a victim from another pimp, or what a girl must pay to leave a pimp (often dangerous or impossible due to debt bondage).
15. Breaking / Seasoning – The intentional use of trauma, rape, violence, or degradation to "break" a victim's will and make them more compliant.
16. Track / Blade / Stroll – Street terms for areas where prostitution and trafficking activity is concentrated. For example: "She's out on the blade tonight."
17. Daddy / Poppa – A term many victims are forced to use to refer to their pimp or trafficker, creating psychological dependence and distorted attachment.
18. Square / Green – Someone who is not part of "the life" (i.e., trafficking or street culture). Often used to describe people who don't understand pimp culture.
19. Game / The Life – The culture, rules, and lifestyle of prostitution and trafficking. Survivors often refer to being "in the life" or "leaving the game."
20. Trap House / Spot – A place where victims are kept, often against their will, and where buyers

come for sexual exploitation. This location is a place where drugs are sold as well.

HOW DO TRAFFICKERS FIND NEW VICTIMS?

Traffickers often use online platforms to research and target their victims. They may set up fake profiles on social media, dating sites, and gaming systems to gain the trust of their victims. In-person, traffickers look for vulnerabilities and traumas to exploit. They seek to fill a need in the grooming process so that they can make their new victim believe that they are indebted to them and demand sexual acts for repayment. Traffickers also look for individuals who are easy to manipulate and control, such as run-aways, foster children, people struggling with sub-stance abuse, international immigrant workers, and students. By filling a perceived need—love, safety, opportunity—traffickers create a false sense of in-debtedness and control.

RED FLAGS TO SHARE WITH OTHERS

1. Dreams being sold to you that seem too good to be true: Traffickers often offer their victims the promise of a better life, such as a job op-portunity or a chance to travel to a new city or country. These offers can be very attractive and lure unsuspecting individuals into a dangerous situation.
2. New "friends" online: Traffickers use social media and other online platforms to find and

target potential victims. They may use fake pro-files to befriend individuals and gain their trust. Service providers need to be aware of this and promote online safety by encouraging people to be cautious when accepting friend requests and to limit personal information that is shared online.

3. A free one-way ticket being given to you for a fun trip or business opportunity: Traffickers often lure their victims by offering them a free trip or a job opportunity, but once they arrive at the destination, they are forced into trafficking.

4. Someone much older, whom you don't real-ly know, taking an interest in dating you and spoiling you with lots of free stuff: Traffickers often manipulate their victims by pretending to be in a romantic relationship with them. They shower them with gifts and compliments to create a sense of dependence and attachment.

5. When someone tries to isolate you from family and friends to convince you to be in a rela-tionship solely dependent on them: Traffickers often use isolation as a tactic to control their victims. They may convince them to cut off contact with their family and friends, making them more vulnerable to exploitation.

6. Anytime you get into drugs: Traffickers often use drugs to control their victims, making them more compliant and easier to manipulate. The drug trade is also often connected to sex trafficking.

7. Underage drinking at parties: Young people are often targeted by traffickers at parties where they may be drugged, raped, and exploited.
8. A new job that pressures you to quickly relocate: Traffickers often offer jobs that require their victims to move to a new city or country, making it harder for them to escape.
9. Abusive relationships can also potentially lead to sexual exploitation: Abusive partners may use coercion or violence to force their victims into sex acts with others, for their financial gain. This is trafficking.
10. Being in a relationship with someone addicted to pornography is a risk: Pornography addiction can lead to a desire to act out fantasies in real life, and victims may be forced into sexual acts they are uncomfortable with.
11. Being lured to catch a ride with a stranger: Traffickers may offer their victims a ride, and once they are in the car, they are forced into slavery.
12. Running away from home puts you at risk: Runaway youth are often targeted by traffickers who offer them a place to stay, food, and money, only to exploit them later.

HOW TO EDUCATE MINORS ABOUT TRAFFICKING

One of the most common questions I hear from parents and caregivers is, "How do I talk to my child about trafficking?" As a survivor and someone who's worked closely with exploited minors, I've seen first-hand how vital it is to create a home environment free from shame and judgment. When kids and teens know that they can come to you without fear of punishment or overreaction, they're more likely to share when something feels off or unsafe.

Imagine your child encountering something disturbing online or in person. If they know they can tell you about a creepy message or a scary encounter without getting in trouble, they'll come to you. For example, if they come to you to get help because a nasty man sent them a picture of their genitalia through social media, would you take their phone and punish them? Or would you help navigate the situation, providing steps of safety without punishing them for their vulnerability and openness with you? That open line of communication can make all the difference in protecting them from predators.

When you talk about trafficking, do it in a way that empowers rather than terrifies. Help them understand that there are people out there who might pretend to be kind but have bad intentions—people who want to use others' bodies for their own financial gain. By educating them about red flags and encouraging them to trust their instincts, you equip them with the tools to stay safe.

Also, consider implementing practical safety measures, such as parental control apps and having a pre-arranged code word or emoji for emergencies. This way, your child can signal for help discreetly if they ever feel unsafe. And remember, the goal is to create a culture of trust and openness, where your child knows they can always come to you for support and prayer, without fear of judgment.

IDENTIFYING VICTIMS

Some identifiers that may indicate a person is a victim of trafficking include:

1. A reluctance to make eye contact: Trafficking victims may avoid making eye contact, which can be a sign of fear or shame.
2. Another person speaking for them: If someone else is speaking for the person, it may indicate that they're not in control of their own life.
3. Lack of control over identification: If a person doesn't have control over their identification documents or other personal information, it could be a sign of trafficking.
4. Tattoos or branding: Traffickers may brand their victims with tattoos, which can serve as a sign of ownership.
5. Scripted or rehearsed responses: Victims may be coached on what to say and how to act in order to avoid detection.
6. Signs of physical abuse: Unexplained bruises or other injuries may be a sign of physical abuse.
7. Submissive or fearful: Trafficking victims may be fearful or overly submissive, particularly around their traffickers.
8. Appearing destitute/lacking personal possessions: Victims may not have personal possessions or money of their own.

9. Working excessively long hours: Victims may work long hours with no breaks or time off.
10. Living with their employer or at their job: Trafficking victims may live with their traffickers or be forced to live on the premises where they work.

It's important to note that any child or teen involved in the sex industry is a victim of trafficking, regardless of whether or not they exhibit the above identifiers. It's crucial that service providers remain alert and vigilant in their efforts to identify and assist victims of sex trafficking.

STATEMENTS SURVIVORS MAY MAKE BEFORE REALIZING THEY WERE TRAFFICKED

Many victims of sex trafficking do not self-identify as victims—especially in the early stages of recovery or disclosure. This is often due to deeply ingrained shame, confusion, and psychological manipulation. Some may still blame themselves for what happened, believing they were complicit or that it was "just abuse" rather than trafficking. Others may not yet recognize that the person who exploited them was a trafficker—especially when a trauma bond has been formed. These internal conflicts, combined with cultural narratives and a lack of accurate language, can make it difficult for survivors to see their experiences clearly.

- "I used to have a sugar daddy who paid my bills, but sometimes he'd loan me out to his friends when I couldn't keep up."
- "I thought we were just making content together for OnlyFans, but then he started forcing me to do things on camera I didn't agree to."
- "I was sexually abused. When I lived with my aunt and uncle, their friends would come over and 'babysit' me. They always gave my uncle cash."
- "I met a guy online who said he loved me. He flew me out, but once I got there, he took my phone and made me start working at a club."
- "My mom told me it was just something our family did to survive. She said I owed it to her to help pay the rent."
- "I thought I was working as an escort to support myself, but my manager kept all the money and said I had to work it off."
- "When I ran away, I didn't have anywhere to go. This older guy let me stay with him, but then he started bringing guys over."
- "I used to hang out at parties where the older guys would drug us and pass us around. I just thought that's what happened when you partied too hard."
- "At first, I wanted to dance to make money, but then my boyfriend said if I loved him, I'd do extras in the backroom for his cut."
- "I was convinced to be in a poly relationship. He said it was spiritual and freeing, but I was the

only one he made sleep with other people for money."

- "My foster dad used to say I was his favorite. He gave me gifts, but only if I let him do things to me. He recorded it and let his friends watch."
- "We were part of a church that had secret rituals. I didn't think it was wrong until I got older and realized I was being touched by grown men during them."
- "My trafficker said it wasn't trafficking because I said yes. But I only said yes because I was scared of what would happen if I didn't."

NOTES

CHAPTER 2

UNDERSTANDING THE PSYCHOLOGY OF TRAFFICKERS

While many view traffickers as pure predators, it's important to understand that many traffickers were once victims themselves. A significant number of traffickers, especially those operating in familial or generational trafficking rings, were sexually abused as children. This unhealed trauma can fester into cycles of control, power-seeking, and exploitation of others. Rather than confronting their pain, some choose to reenact it, turning their own victimization into a strategy for dominance.

In addition to personal histories of abuse, traffickers often emerge from environments where the exploitation of women and children has been normalized. Cultural messages—particularly in music, pornography, and media—glorify pimp culture, hypersexualize children, and desensitize audiences to violence and domination. Songs that praise the power of the "pimp" and reduce women to sexual objects aren't just entertainment; they are programming. These messages reinforce the narcissistic worldview of traffickers, who often justify their actions by convincing themselves that their victims "want it," "chose this life," or "owe them."

Moreover, when society sexualizes children through fashion trends, viral content, and lenient legal frameworks, it creates fertile ground for exploitation. The trafficker's grooming becomes easier in a world already primed to see minors as mature or sexually available. For this reason, it is crucial to expose not only individual trafficking cases, but also the broader cultural frameworks that support and sustain them.

Understanding these factors doesn't excuse traffickers' actions, but it equips us to disrupt the root systems and societal structures that breed exploitation. True justice and prevention come not only through legal intervention, but through cultural repentance and transformation. As we dismantle these mindsets, we also pave the way for healing—not just for victims, but potentially even for former perpetrators willing to confront their brokenness, repent, and convert their lives to faith in Jesus.

We are living in a day and time when not only are our children being sexualized, but there is a growing agenda to protect those who seek to abuse and exploit them. It is a grotesque and evil distortion to frame pedophilia as a "sexual preference" worthy of protection or acceptance. This ideology is not only from the pit of hell, but it endangers children and empowers predators. No individual who tolerates or normalizes this thinking can truly claim to value justice or innocence.

TRAFFICKERS ARE NARCISSISTS

Understanding the psychology of traffickers is crucial for recognizing the dynamics at play in sex trafficking. Most traffickers exhibit strong narcissistic traits, using coercive control, psychological warfare, and manipulation to dominate their victims. These tactics mirror those identified in Biderman's Chart of Coercion, which outlines methods like isolation, monopolizing perception, induced exhaustion, threats, occasional kindness, demonstrating control, humiliation, and trivial demands. These methods, originally documented in studies of prisoners of war, highlight how traffickers systematically break down their victims' will and sense of self.

TYPES OF NARCISSISTIC TRAFFICKERS

- Covert Narcissists (The "Romeo" Trafficker): These traffickers often appear charming, loving, and supportive, winning the trust of their victims and those around them. Publicly, they may seem like the perfect partner or friend, but behind closed doors, they are emotionally and psychologically manipulative, using affection as a tool of control.

- Overt Narcissists (The "Gorilla" Trafficker): These traffickers are openly domineering and abusive. They rely on intimidation, physical violence, and threats to maintain power and control. They often display grandiose self-importance, entitlement, and lack empathy for others.

- Malignant Narcissists ("Familial" Trafficking): In cases of familial trafficking, the traffickers often exhibit malignant narcissism, which combines extreme narcissistic traits with aggression, sadism, and a complete lack of empathy. These traffickers may be parents or relatives who exploit the child for financial gain, power, or other benefits. They often operate under a veil of secrecy and manipulation, making it incredibly difficult for the victim to recognize the abuse. This type of trafficker can also exhibit covert narcissistic traits, presenting themselves as caring or victimized to outsiders while secretly abusing and exploiting the child. The betrayal of trust in a familial context makes this form of trafficking especially insidious and damaging.

KEY NARCISSISTIC ABUSE TACTICS

- Love Bombing: At the beginning of the relationship, traffickers may overwhelm their victims with flattery, affection, attention, and gifts. This grooming and intense display of false "love" creates an emotional high and a sense of loyalty. Once attachment is formed, the trafficker begins to devalue, manipulate, and exploit the victim.

- Gaslighting: This tactic involves causing the victim to doubt their memories, perceptions, or sanity. Traffickers use gaslighting to disorient their victims and make them feel dependent and confused. Gaslighting is master manipulation and conditioning/programming. The victim is always wrong and the trafficker is always right. An individual can gaslight without even realizing it, especially when they are desperate to protect their narrative and avoid accountability. In doing so, they instinctively shift blame onto the victim, justifying their abuse and reinforcing control.

- Smear Campaigns: Traffickers often spread lies or distorted narratives about their victims to others. This damages the victim's reputation, isolates them from support systems, and makes it more difficult for them to seek help or be believed.

- Flying Monkeys: Traffickers may use others to do their bidding and enforce control over the victim. These "flying monkeys" can be friends, relatives, or even strangers who believe the trafficker's version of events. They help reinforce the trafficker's narrative, further isolating and controlling the victim. In some cases, this includes the trafficker's own parents or family members, making the survivor feel outnumbered, invalidated, and trapped. Flying Monkeys often use gaslighting tactics as well to protect the pimp or trafficker.

By understanding these dynamics, survivors and those supporting them can better recognize the signs of narcissistic abuse and gain insight into the psychological control that often keeps victims bound. It's also important to recognize that prolonged exposure to such abuse can lead survivors to develop antisocial behaviors or coping mechanisms that were necessary for survival. These learned behaviors can be misunderstood if not seen through a trauma-informed lens.

For service providers and compassionate individuals working with survivors, it's essential to help them identify patterns of narcissistic abuse—not just from traffickers, but also in future relationships. Some survivors may feel tempted to tolerate a toxic relationship if it seems "not as bad" as their trafficking experience. But emotional and psychological abuse in any form is still abuse. Helping survivors understand the full spectrum of narcissistic manipulation empowers them to set boundaries, rebuild their self-worth, and avoid repeating patterns of exploitation.

Recognizing that traffickers' behavior stems from a distorted self-perception and need for control, not anything the victim did, also helps dismantle the shame survivors may carry. The abuse they endured was never their fault.

NOTES

CHAPTER 3

INTERACTING WITH POTENTIAL VICTIMS

When working with potential victims of sex trafficking, it's important to approach every interaction with sensitivity, empathy, and a victim-centered approach. Trauma-informed care should be the guiding principle in all interactions, and this includes prioritizing the victim's safety and well-being, building trust, offering choices, collaborating with them, and empowering them.

To establish a safe and trusting relationship with the victim, service providers should ensure that the victim feels safe and secure. They should also be compassionate, caring, and follow through on their promises to build trust with the victim. Providing options and letting the victim make choices demonstrates that you value their thoughts and feelings and is a key component of trauma-informed care.

This is why it is harmful to pressure a survivor to engage in conversations about religion or faith if they are not ready. For many individuals, this can feel like judgment, manipulation, or control. While you may be open about your values or background, ultimately, the individual's autonomy and readiness must be respected. Pressuring a survivor in any direction—spiritually or otherwise—can fracture trust. Victims are often observing service providers closely to assess safety, sincerity, and whether the support offered is free from conditions or hidden expectations.

When communicating with potential victims, it's important to stay safe and be aware that the trafficker may be watching or listening. You should speak to them one-on-one and express care and concern, while also being non-judgmental and respectful of their choices. It's crucial to stay positive, patient, and avoid making promises that cannot be kept.

Service providers should also be mindful of not trying to fix or diagnose the victim's trauma, as this can be disempowering and may not be helpful. Instead, they should be active listeners, providing emotional support, and empowering the victim to make decisions about their own healing journey.

To assess whether a person is a victim of sex trafficking, the U.S. Department of State suggests asking specific questions related to their work, freedom of movement, and personal circumstances. These questions can help identify signs of coercion, exploitation, or control, and can inform appropriate interventions:

- Can you leave your job if you want to?
- Can you come and go as you please?

- Have you been hurt or threatened if you tried to leave?
- Has your family been threatened?
- Do you live with your employer?
- Where do you sleep and eat?
- Are you in debt to your employer?
- Do you have your passport/identification? Who has it?

Ultimately, interacting with potential victims of sex trafficking requires compassion, sensitivity, and a trauma-informed approach. By building trust, empowering the victim, and offering support, service providers can help survivors recover and move forward with their lives.

WHY VICTIMS DON'T WANT TO TALK TO YOU

"Building rapport is the first step in interviewing victims in a trauma-informed way. It is critical to keep in mind that a victim's reality is your reality when preparing for and conducting investigative interviews with potential trafficking victims... Law enforcement task force members need to be mindful that human trafficking investigations are purposely victim-centered because the victim supplies the most critical evidence—personal testimony—if there is a trial. However, victims must be stabilized both mentally and physically and must feel safe before investigators can begin in-depth interviews, and service providers and civil attorneys can provide essential support."

—Office for Victims of Crime. (n.d.). Human Trafficking Task Force E-Guide. [Online]. Available: https://www.ovcttac.gov/task-forceguide [Accessed: March 30, 2023].

Sex trafficking victims may struggle to communicate with service providers for various reasons, and it is essential to understand these reasons to provide effective support and assistance. Some of the reasons that victims may not want to talk include:

1. Trauma – Victims have experienced severe trauma, and talking about it can be incredibly triggering and overwhelming. They may have anxiety or panic attacks just to meet with service providers, unsure of what they will have to relive by talking about the trauma.

2. Triggering environment – Some victims may find it difficult to talk in certain locations or environments, especially if something in the room reminds them of their trauma.

3. Feeling judged and misunderstood – Victims may feel judged and misunderstood by service providers, especially if they have had negative experiences in the past.

4. Fear of being a "snitch" – Victims may feel like service providers just want information and do not actually care about them or what happens to them after they give the information.

5. Lack of safety – Victims may not feel safe around service providers, especially if they have had to provide sex acts for people in the same profession during their trafficking.

6. Fractured memory – Some victims may have suppressed traumatic memories, making it difficult for them to remember details or to acknowledge that something happened.
7. Fear of retaliation – Victims may be terrified that their trafficker will find out they told someone and that there will be severe consequences.
8. Paranoia – Victims may be paranoid that service providers could be working with their trafficker, even in the justice system.
9. Code words – Service providers may use certain words or phrases that trigger victims or remind them of their trauma.
10. Communication style – Service providers may come across as too aggressive, forceful, or lacking compassion, making it difficult for victims to feel comfortable talking.
11. Lack of advocacy – Victims may not have an advocate or trusted person with them to comfort them through the process and stick up for them if they are triggered or mishandled.
12. Broken promises – Service providers may have made promises that they did not follow through on, leading to mistrust and reluctance to talk.
13. Using pet names – Service providers using pet names like "Honey" or "Sweetie" can be a trigger for victims, reminding them of names their traffickers and customers used.
14. Fake safe people – Someone around the victim may be faking that they are a safe person, but they are loyal to the trafficker or cult and will report back

15. Dissociative Identity Disorder (DID) – If the victim has DID, a protector or cult-loyal alter/part may be leading, making it difficult for them to communicate with service providers.
16. Emotional distress – Victims may be having a triggering and emotional day, making it challenging to communicate.
17. Fear of consequences – Victims may be scared that they will get in trouble or lose support if they tell the truth about what is going on.
18. Lack of trust – Victims may not trust service providers due to negative past experiences.
19. Personal choice – Finally, victims may simply not feel like talking or may not be ready to talk about their experiences.

It is crucial to be compassionate, kind, and caring when communicating with victims and survivors of sex trafficking. Individuals on the front lines of the fight against trafficking should understand that it may take time for victims to open up and that each person's journey is unique. It is important to create a safe and supportive environment and to offer resources and assistance at a pace that is comfortable for the victim.

Please make space for this reality during intake processes. For example, do not pressure a survivor to share details of their trafficking experience if they are not ready or do not have adequate support in place to process the emotions that often follow disclosure.

NOTES

CHAPTER 4

UNDERSTANDING THE INTERNAL WAR OF
TRAFFICKING VICTIMS

Sex trafficking victims often experience significant trauma, which can impact them in numerous ways. The effects of trauma are not limited to one area of life, as they can show up physically, mentally, emotionally, spiritually, and behaviorally. It's important to understand how complex trauma affects the whole person—body, mind, and emotions.

Misinterpreting a survivor's behavior or symptoms can cause additional harm. For instance, if someone is battling depression, it may not be rooted in something spiritual, but instead may be the result of a hormonal or chemical imbalance, emotional suppression, or prolonged psychological stress. Labeling survivors inaccurately can leave them feeling judged, misunderstood, and more hopeless than before.

Instead, service providers should focus on meeting survivors with respect, patience, and clinical discernment, aiming to support their healing holistically. The goal is to help survivors move toward wholeness through informed care, not quick assumptions.

COMMON QUESTIONS ASKED

- Why don't they leave their trafficker?
- Why do they protect their pimp?
- Why won't they just say they are a victim?
- Why won't they report their abuse?
- Why do some girls return to their pimp after escape or being rescued?

STOCKHOLM SYNDROME

Stockholm Syndrome, trauma bonding, and complex trauma are all very real experiences that sex trafficking victims may face. These phenomena can be difficult to understand, but service providers need to have a basic understanding of these concepts to provide appropriate care and support.

Stockholm Syndrome is a psychological condition in which a victim develops feelings of trust or affection toward their abuser. In sex trafficking situations, this can occur when a victim believes that their trafficker is protecting or helping them in some way. This response is not a conscious decision but a survival mechanism developed under extreme stress and fear.

TRAUMA BONDING

Trauma bonding occurs when a victim forms an emotional attachment to their trafficker due to intermittent abuse, manipulation, and perceived care or affection. Cultural beliefs about loyalty or debt, along with cycles of kindness followed by violence, contribute to this bond. Victims may believe they are in love with their abuser, even defending them. Recognizing trauma bonding as a survival strategy is essential to understanding why a victim might return or hesitate to leave.

COMPLEX TRAUMA

Complex trauma refers to repeated or prolonged exposure to traumatic events, especially those involving betrayal, captivity, and powerlessness. Sex trafficking victims are often subjected to multiple layers of abuse including fear, coercion, addiction, sexual violence, and psychological manipulation. The impacts of this trauma can manifest as anxiety, depression, dissociation (including Dissociative Identity Disorder), unexplained pain, and suicidal thoughts.

FEAR

One of the most common reasons survivors stay with traffickers is fear—often based on real threats. Traffickers use violence, intimidation, and threats against the victim or their loved ones to enforce compliance.

These threats are often credible and terrifying, making escape feel impossible.

DEBT BONDAGE

Traffickers may fabricate or inflate debts that the victim "owes" them. These debts can feel insurmountable and are often enforced through manipulation or violence. Even when not legal or legitimate, victims may believe they must repay these debts or suffer severe consequences.

ADDICTION / SUBSTANCE ABUSE

Substance use is commonly intertwined with sex trafficking. Traffickers may use drugs to create dependency and maintain control. Drugs may be introduced during the "breaking in" process, and victims may use substances to numb the emotional and physical pain of exploitation. When drugs wear off, trauma symptoms can become more intense, making recovery even more difficult without support.

Fear, debt bondage, and addiction are deeply interconnected, often trapping victims in cycles of exploitation. Raising awareness and equipping service providers to respond with compassion and understanding is critical. Providers should understand phenomena like Stockholm Syndrome, trauma bonding, and complex trauma, and tailor care accordingly. Trauma-informed therapy, safety planning, and referrals to specialized services are often necessary.

TRAUMA, SYMPTOMS, AND BEHAVIORS

Survivors of sex trafficking endure complex and pro-longed trauma. Their symptoms may be difficult to understand, but they are valid, and often linked to both neurological and psychological impacts. Below are common trauma-related responses:

1. Complex Post-Traumatic Stress Disorder (C-PTSD): Persistent emotional dysregulation, shame, difficulty trusting, intrusive flashbacks, dissociation, hypervigilance, nightmares, and a fragmented sense of self.
2. Anxiety and panic attacks: Often triggered by memories, sensory cues, or fear of danger.
3. Avoidance, disorientation, phobias: Difficulty functioning or feeling grounded in everyday life.
4. Emotional triggers and flashbacks: Survivors may re-experience intense emotional states without conscious recall of the original event.
5. Dissociation or immobility: Survivors may freeze, check out, or feel disconnected from their body or surroundings.
6. Depression and hopelessness: Persistent sadness, crying spells, or emotional numbness.
7. Suppressed memories and time loss: Survivors may not recall large parts of their life, especially abuse-related events.
8. Dissociative Disorders: Including Dissociative Identity Disorder, where alternate parts may carry trauma memories or protective functions.

9. Distrust of law enforcement: Due to past criminalization or being assaulted by individuals in positions of authority.
10. Normalization of exploitation: Survivors may not recognize their experience as abuse if it has become their "normal."
11. Sleep disturbances: Including nightmares and insomnia.
12. Feelings of inferiority and shame: Survivors may view themselves as "damaged" or unworthy of connection.
13. Difficulty concentrating or remembering: Common effects of trauma on cognitive function.
14. Self-harm and suicidal ideation: Often driven by unresolved trauma or a desire to escape pain.
15. Sexual dysfunction or hypersexuality: Sexual trauma can lead to numbness or compulsive behaviors.
16. Fear of strangers or unfamiliar environments.
17. Anger and irritability: Especially when survivors feel trapped, misunderstood, or controlled.
18. Isolation: Survivors may withdraw socially or avoid supportive relationships.
19. Changes in eating patterns or eating disorders.
20. Bathroom-related challenges: Including constipation or trouble urinating, often related to pelvic trauma, chronic stress, or dissociation.
21. Satanic Ritual Abuse (SRA): Some survivors may have experienced exploitation connected to ritualistic abuse. This can involve extreme trauma, fragmentation of identity, and deep layers of psychological and spiritual manipulation.

THE NEUROBIOLOGY OF TRAUMA

The trauma experienced by sex trafficking survivors deeply impacts the brain and nervous system. Key areas involved include:

- Amygdala: The brain's fear center, responsible for detecting danger and triggering emotional reactions. Survivors may have heightened reactivity or emotional outbursts tied to trauma triggers.
- Hippocampus: Involved in memory formation. Survivors may have fragmented, distorted, or incomplete memories due to the effects of trauma on this region.
- Prefrontal Cortex: Responsible for decision-making and rational thought. Trauma can reduce this area's function, impairing the ability to assess risk, plan, or make safe choices.

These brain changes are not a sign of weakness or instability—they are the body's way of surviving in overwhelming situations. Understanding this can help service providers validate survivor experiences and advocate for them in legal, medical, or therapeutic settings.

Survivors may engage in behaviors that seem irrational, contradictory, or detached from reality—but these are often neurobiological responses to trauma. Providers, advocates, and legal professionals may consider partnering with trauma-informed therapists or expert witnesses who can speak to these brain changes in court when needed.

NOTES

CHAPTER 5

DISSOCIATION

Sex trafficking is a form of trauma that can cause severe dissociation in its victims. Dissociation is a coping mechanism that the brain uses to protect itself from overwhelming or traumatic experiences. In the case of sex trafficking, dissociation can occur in many different ways.

One common form of dissociation that sex trafficking victims experience is depersonalization. This involves feeling detached from one's body, thoughts, and emotions, as if observing them from a distance. Victims may feel like they are watching themselves being abused rather than experiencing the abuse directly. This can help them feel less pain and distress during the abuse, but it can also lead to a sense of disconnection from their own body, identity, and emotions afterward.

Another form of dissociation that sex trafficking victims may experience is dissociative amnesia. This involves blocking out memories of traumatic experiences, either partially or completely. Victims may have gaps in their memory or may forget entire periods of time. This can make it difficult for them to process and heal from their experiences, as they may not have a complete understanding of what happened to them.

Dissociative Identity Disorder (DID), formerly known as multiple personality disorder, is another dissociative disorder that can develop as a result of sex trafficking. DID involves the presence of two or more distinct personality states, each with its own way of perceiving, relating to, and thinking about the world. DID can develop as a way of coping with severe and ongoing abuse, allowing the victim to compartmentalize and create distinct identities to help them survive.

DID is typically diagnosed through clinical assessments using tools such as the Structured Clinical Interview for DSM-5 Dissociative Disorders (SCID-D) or the Dissociative Experiences Scale (DES). However, if an alter or internal part presents as highly functional, the survivor may not be accurately diagnosed. Many survivors learn to protect their inner system and may not reveal dissociative symptoms unless they feel completely safe and understood.

Some survivors may describe having "parts" of themselves or internal voices that resemble the model of Internal Family Systems (IFS). Whether or not they have a clinical diagnosis of DID, survivors may benefit from support that acknowledges the presence of internal dynamics, such as younger or protective parts. Recognizing and respecting these parts can be an important element of trauma recovery.

It is important to note that not all survivors of sex trafficking experience dissociation, and those who do may experience it in different ways. Dissociation is also not exclusive to trafficking survivors and can occur in people who have experienced other types of trauma.

Understanding the various types of dissociation that sex trafficking survivors may experience is crucial for service providers. It helps build patience, compassion, and more effective support strategies. With the right care and resources, survivors can recover from dissociation and trauma-related mental health conditions.

THE WORDS OF SEX TRAFFICKING SURVIVORS WHO EXPERIENCED DISSOCIATION

In a study on the prostitution and trafficking of women and children in Minnesota, survivors described how dissociation helped them endure their exploitation:

"If you're having sex with someone you don't want to, you leave."

"When the johns were sexually assaulting me, I could be in England or somewhere else until they were done."

"There's times I'd walk around in a space-out because when I stop and think about reality, I break down and can't handle it."

"[Dissociation is] cutting myself off from my body. I think of it like a game. Then it's [the prostitution] done and over with."

"It's a way of blocking memories...leading a double life within."

Several women spoke of learning to dissociate during childhood sexual abuse:

"I learned how to do that [dissociate] when I was a child being raped."

"When I was nine years old and being raped, my mind left my body and was looking down from the ceiling..."

"Dissociation permits psychological survival, whether the traumatic event(s) are slavery, military combat, incest, or prostitution. It is an elaborate escape and avoidance strategy in which overwhelming human cruelty results in fragmentation of the mind into different parts that observe, react, or do not know about the harm."

—Farley, M. et al. (2011), *Garden of Truth*

STATEMENTS DISSOCIATED / FRACTURED SURVIVORS MIGHT MAKE

Disclaimer: The following statements are for educational purposes only. They are not intended to diagnose DID or any other condition. They are shared to foster trauma-informed understanding and sensitivity.

1. During a traumatic experience, I check out and disconnect.
2. I often feel numb or detached from my own emotions, body, or surroundings.
3. I can mentally escape when feeling triggered or threatened.
4. I hear different voices inside that feel like younger or other versions of me.
5. I have difficulty maintaining healthy relationships due to emotional distance.
6. I have moments of not feeling like myself.
7. I have huge memory gaps or missing time.
8. I feel disconnected from everything around me.
9. I feel like I'm watching my life from the outside.
10. Sometimes I feel like I'm in a dream or fog.
11. I don't recognize myself in the mirror.
12. I go through the motions but feel disconnected.
13. I can't recall key events or details from my past.
14. My emotions feel blocked or locked away.
15. Sometimes I don't feel in control of my actions.
16. I feel disconnected from my body, like I'm floating.
17. It's hard to know if some memories are real.
18. I experience sudden mood or personality shifts.
19. I go on autopilot and lose track of time.
20. I struggle with identity confusion.
21. My brain gets foggy, and I can't hold conversations.
22. I feel like parts of me are stuck in trauma memories.
23. Items in my home move or disappear, and I don't remember doing it.

Survivors of sex trafficking often face intense emotional, psychological, and physical challenges when engaging with systems of care, legal processes, and services that require disclosure or vulnerability. Having a trained advocate—especially one with lived experience or trauma-informed training—can be invaluable during these moments. Whether accompanying a survivor through a SANE exam, sitting with them before or after giving victim testimony in court, supporting them during law enforcement interviews, or helping them navigate medical or mental health evaluations, advocates play a critical role in helping survivors stay grounded and present. Their presence can reduce dissociation, mitigate fear, and provide emotional regulation tools in real time. Other examples of high-stress scenarios where advocates are essential include child welfare investigations, immigration screenings, probation check-ins, emergency room visits, shelter intake, or even simply returning to locations where trauma occurred. Felt safety is the foundation of trauma-informed care, and advocates help create that safety by offering consistent, compassionate presence—empowering the survivor while also allowing service providers to achieve their objectives more effectively and ethically.

NOTES

PART TWO: SATANIC RITUAL ABUSE / OCCULT TRAFFICKING

CHAPTER 6

INTRODUCTION TO SRA AND SEX
TRAFFICKING

A NOTE BEFORE YOU BEGIN

This section addresses deeply challenging and heavy topics. While the content may be difficult to process, it is essential for a comprehensive understanding of the realities many survivors face. I encourage you to read through with the knowledge that this chapter concludes on a note of empowerment and hope.

LET'S BEGIN

"~20% of the survivors of sex trafficking who seek help with escape have satanic ritual abuse in their exploitation history."

-Rescue America

We are living in a pivotal moment, one that mirrors the national shift that began over two decades ago when the United States first started to define and address sex trafficking with clarity and urgency. In 2000, the United States passed the Trafficking Victims Protection Act (TVPA), the first comprehensive federal law to combat human trafficking, including sex trafficking. At that time, survivors were often misidentified as criminals and labeled as prostitutes, addicts, or runaways. There were no federal protections in place, no reliable data being collected, and very few systems equipped to hold traffickers accountable. Much of this failure stemmed from asking the wrong questions. It took courageous survivors and dedicated advocates to shift the narrative and awaken the nation to what was really happening.

Today, we are experiencing a similar wave of awakening—this time surrounding the issue of Satanic Ritual Abuse (SRA). Just as it once was with sex trafficking, most people are only now beginning to understand the realities of ritual abuse and its deep ties to organized trafficking networks. In 2025, Utah passed House Bill 66, known as the "Ritual Abuse Amendments," officially recognizing ritual abuse of a child as a second-degree felony. The law defines specific acts—including animal sacrifice, ingestion of bodily fluids, mock ceremonies, and spiritual manipulation—as components of ritual abuse. It also mandates specialized training for law enforcement to help identify indicators of ritual abuse in sexual assault investigations. This groundbreaking legislation represents the first of its kind in the United

States and signals a growing national shift toward awareness, accountability, and justice for survivors.

Service providers who work with survivors of sex trafficking must understand the dynamics of ritual abuse and be equipped to serve these individuals with compassion, professionalism, and trauma-informed care—free from judgment or disbelief.

KEY TERMS: UNDERSTANDING THE LANGUAGE OF SRA

Before we explore the complex and often hidden realities of Satanic Ritual Abuse (SRA), it's important to define a few core terms. These brief explanations will help ground your understanding as we move through survivor testimonies, historical research, biblical insight, and spiritual principles.

SPIRITUAL ABUSE

Spiritual abuse is the misuse of religious authority, doctrine, or practices to control, manipulate, shame, or harm others. It often involves physical or sexual abuse that is justified or excused through distorted interpretations of scripture, religious roles, or divine will. This type of abuse may occur in churches, religious institutions, or other faith-based communities, where leaders or members use spiritual beliefs to silence victims, demand submission, sexually abuse, or coerce obedience. Survivors of spiritual abuse may struggle with deep confusion, mistrust of religious environments, and feelings of shame, guilt, or fear tied to their faith.

SATANIC RITUAL ABUSE (SRA)

Satanic Ritual Abuse is a highly organized and spiritually charged form of abuse that involves sexual, physical, psychological, and spiritual trauma. It is typically carried out by cults or groups who worship Satan or demonic entities. SRA often includes rituals, sacrifices, blood covenants, and programming methods designed to fracture the soul and create dissociated "parts" or alternate personalities. Many SRA survivors are also victims of familial and sex trafficking networks, where the abuse begins in early childhood and continues through ritual calendars and cult systems of control.

OCCULT CRIMES

Occult crimes refer to criminal acts—such as sexual abuse, human trafficking, ritual sacrifice, or torture—committed in the context of occult practices. These crimes are often committed by individuals or groups who believe in esoteric, mystical, or satanic power structures, including some secret societies, witchcraft covens, and Satanic cults. Occult crimes often involve symbols, rituals, coded language, spiritual contracts, and desecration of the human body for perceived supernatural gain.

MIND CONTROL PROGRAMMING

Mind control programming is the systematic use of trauma, repetition, and spiritual manipulation to fracture the human mind and create dissociated identities (also called "alters" or parts). These parts are then programmed with specific codes, phrases, roles, or triggers to ensure obedience and secrecy. This method, often beginning in early childhood, may include extreme torture, hypnosis, drugs, rituals, and sexual abuse. Many survivors of SRA report programming that mirrors known government projects like MK Ultra, which used similar methods to create highly controlled individuals for exploitation and covert operations.

HISTORICAL ROOTS AND MODERN EXPRESSIONS

Satanic Ritual Abuse (SRA) is a controversial and often misunderstood topic, but it is a real phenomenon that has affected many individuals. It is a form of extreme abuse involving physical, sexual, spiritual, and emotional trauma, often in the context of a cult or group that worships Satan or other malevolent entities.

Many victims report being abused and trafficked by individuals in religious cults, Satanism, witchcraft groups, and occult-based secret societies. Not all members of these religious groups are involved in trafficking; however, survivors frequently identify high-ranking members of these cults as perpetrators.

Lower-level participants may or may not be aware of the trafficking activities.

To understand the most hidden and complex forms of sex trafficking, it is essential to understand SRA. Whether or not someone believes these testimonies, the survivors' realities must be honored. Within their stories may lie critical intelligence that could dismantle trafficking networks.

It's important to recognize that SRA involves ancient patterns of ritual abuse that continue in modern times. Notorious gangs and cartels, such as MS-13 and various satanic-affiliated criminal networks, are known to engage in human sacrifices and ritual abuse as part of their exploitation of both minors and adults. These groups perpetuate the same horrific practices described throughout history, underscoring that the battle against ritual abuse and occult crimes is not confined to the past. Understanding these modern expressions of evil is crucial for those committed to bringing healing and freedom to survivors today.

SRA TRAFFICKING IN THE BIBLE: EXPOSING THE ANCIENT ROOTS OF RITUAL ABUSE AND OCCULT CRIMES

Satanic Ritual Abuse (SRA) is not a new phenomenon. It is an ancient practice, seen throughout both biblical history and world cultures, cloaked under the names of idolatry, fertility worship, cult prostitution, and temple rituals. The Bible does not shy away from exposing these evil systems and neither should we.

TERMINOLOGY IN ANCIENT CULTIC SYSTEMS

Terms used throughout history for ritualized sex slaves include:

- Temple Prostitute
- Shrine Prostitute
- Sacred Prostitute
- Cult Prostitute
- Hebrew terms: Qadistu, Qedesha, Kedeshah (used for both males and females)

These individuals, many of them children, were dedicated to pagan gods (principalities and demons) by their fathers or temple authorities. They were forced to serve in temple sex rituals, believed to ensure agricultural and economic prosperity. The "worship" was actually demonic ritual abuse, involving sexual exploitation, soul bondage, and spiritual defilement.

"It can be defined narrowly as union with a prostitute... sanctioned by the wardens of a deity... in such cases, the prostitute had semi-official status as a cult functionary... The prostitutes would be slaves owned by the temple."
— Journal of the Evangelical Theological Society, 42.3 (1999)

In other words, many so-called "sacred" prostitutes were trafficked victims, abused in the name of pagan false gods like Baal, Molech, Asherah, and Ishtar.

HISTORICAL CONFIRMATION OF SRA SYSTEMS

- Greek historian Strabo (64 BC–AD 21) wrote about the Temple of Aphrodite in Corinth, which had over 1,000 temple-slaves—both men and women—dedicated to the goddess for ritual sex. "The temple of Aphrodite was so rich that it owned more than a thousand temple-slaves, courtesans (hetairai), whom both women and men had dedicated to the goddess…"— Strabo, Geography
- Herodotus, the "father of history," confirmed that even fathers consecrated their daughters to be used in temple prostitution (sex trafficking), often as a rite of passage.
- Scholar Everett Ferguson writes: "Prostitution became a part of religious rites at certain temples… there were one thousand 'sacred prostitutes' at the temple of Aphrodite at Corinth." — Backgrounds of Early Christianity
- Van der Toorn adds, "When speaking of cultic prostitution, scholars normally refer to religiously legitimated intercourse… The money or the goods received went to the temple funds." — Anchor Bible Dictionary (ABD 5.510)

This is sex trafficking. The victims were forced to do ritual sex acts in obedience to pagan gods, demons, while giving the money to the pagan temples.

SCRIPTURAL EVIDENCE OF RITUAL ABUSE AND CULT PROSTITUTION

The Bible directly references and condemns these evil practices:

Deuteronomy 23:18 (NLT)
"When you are bringing an offering to fulfill a vow, you must not bring to the house of the Lord your God any offering from the earnings of a prostitute, whether a man or a woman, for both are detestable to the Lord your God."

This shows that male and female prostitution tied to religious systems was happening in the biblical era, and God considered it detestable. It was so widespread that God had to bring clear instruction, warning His people not to approach Him with offerings derived from ritual sex acts; acts that were not only abusive but rooted in demonic worship.

Hosea 4:14 (NLT)
"But why should I punish them for their prostitution and adultery? For your men are doing the same thing, sinning with whores and shrine prostitutes. O foolish people! You refuse to understand, so you will be destroyed."

Men of Israel were complicit, participating in shrine prostitution and perpetuating the abuse cycle. God was grieved, not just by the sin, but by the refusal to understand and repent.

Isaiah 57:3–9 (NLT)
This intense prophetic rebuke outlines the depth of Israel's idolatrous rituals—including child sacrifice and spiritual adultery:

"You sacrifice your children down in the valleys... You have committed adultery on every high mountain... You have gone to Molech with olive oil and many perfumes, sending your agents far and wide, even to the world of the dead."

Genesis 38
The story of Tamar and Judah shows that shrine prostitution was known and culturally understood, as Judah mistook Tamar for a shrine prostitute (kedeshah) and offered payment without hesitation.

WHAT DOES THIS MEAN FOR US TODAY?

Satanic Ritual Abuse may be cloaked in modern language and hidden within complex systems, but its core methods and demonic agenda remain the same. What once took place in public temples now operates in secret through underground trafficking networks. Ancient pagan leaders have been replaced by covert operatives within secret societies and high-level systems of power. The enemy's goal has not changed: to dedicate victims to demonic entities, program and control their minds, perform ritual sex acts, and exploit them for money, influence, and spiritual power—all in service to Satan's dark agenda.

WORLD HISTORY - DISSOCIATION, TRAUMA, AND PROGRAMMING

One of the most well-documented and disturbing examples of mind control experimentation is MK Ultra, a covert U.S. government program operated by the CIA from the 1950s through the 1970s. Declassified documents and survivor testimonies reveal that MK Ultra involved non-consensual experiments on civilians, including the use of trauma, drugs, hypnosis, isolation, and electroshock to manipulate and fracture the human mind. While the program was officially shut down, its tactics did not disappear; they evolved. Many survivors of Satanic Ritual Abuse (SRA) describe nearly identical methods of programming and psychological torture, often beginning in early childhood. These survivors report being subjected to intense trauma designed to break down their sense of identity and create dissociated parts (also called "alters") that could be programmed to obey commands without conscious awareness.

MK Ultra programming is closely related to another commonly known government initiative: Operation Paperclip. After World War II, the United States secretly recruited Nazi scientists, including those who had conducted horrific mind control and medical experiments under Adolf Hitler's regime. These individuals were brought into the U.S. through Operation Paperclip to continue their research within government agencies, including the CIA. Many of the techniques used in MK Ultra, such as trauma-based conditioning, hypnosis, drug experimentation, and dissociative programming, are directly linked to the psychological torture and experimentation carried out in Nazi concentration camps. This transfer of knowledge laid the foundation for modern mind control programs, blending scientific manipulation with spiritual and psychological abuse.

Mainstream culture often glorifies and sensationalizes these themes through science fiction, referencing it in films with super soldier themes or characters under government control. However, these depictions are based on chilling truths. For real survivors, these aren't storylines, they're lived experiences. The pain is not symbolic. The programming is real. The spiritual implications are very complex and multifaceted.

People in the anti-trafficking movement must understand the sophisticated and deeply spiritual tactics used by occult traffickers and Satanic Ritual Abuse (SRA) networks to brainwash, control, and spiritually enslave their victims.

One of the most common and sinister methods used is known as "programming" or "conditioning." This involves the repeated use of scripts, stories, chants, and curses spoken over a victim while they are being sexually, physically, emotionally, and spiritually tortured. The goal of this systematic abuse is to cause the victim's mind to dissociate and fracture, creating multiple alter personalities (or "parts") that can be more easily manipulated, assigned roles, and controlled.

In these rituals, trigger codes (specific words, phrases, sounds, and names) are drilled into the fractured mind under extreme duress. Victims are often forced to obey these codes without hesitation. If they disobey or fail to respond, they are subjected to further torture, punishment, or threats against their lives or the lives of others they care about. This instills deep-rooted fear and creates a psychological and spiritual prison that can persist for years.

In addition to spoken code words, symbols, and colors play a major role in programming. Just like code words, they are intentionally used to trigger specific alters, enforce obedience, or reactivate traumatic memories. A victim may be forced to sit in a purple room, for example, while being shown programming videos filled with occult symbols, coded language, and subliminal messages. These carefully curated environments are designed to overwhelm the senses, break down natural resistance, and program the fractured mind to comply. That color then becomes psychologically anchored to the specific trauma and programming experience, making it a powerful tool for future control. When paired with coded instructions, the color alone can trigger compliance from the victim—often without conscious awareness—due to the deep associations formed during the original abuse.

The goal of the programmer is not simply behavioral control; it is spiritual domination. Under torture, the victim is coerced into giving an agreement, permission, or "yes" under extreme duress. This forced consent becomes a legal loophole in the spirit realm, permitting demonic entities to attach to one or more of the fractured soul parts. These parts, now dissociated and enslaved, may become what the occult refers to as "mind control slaves," programmed to perform specific tasks, respond to triggers, or carry out rituals.

Code words, symbols, colors, and even certain music, objects, or smells can be used to access specific alters, assign titles or functions within the cult, or trigger behaviors such as self-harm, dissociation, or returning to the abuser. This makes everyday environments full of potential landmines for survivors. Especially if they have not yet begun the deprogramming, freedom, and healing process.

If programming details ever emerge in a conversation, it is important not to repeat or share those codes with anyone, including well-meaning individuals. Even unintentional exposure to a trigger word or symbol could re-traumatize the survivor or cause an involuntary reaction that leads to harm.

"Ritualistic child abuse is the most hideous of all child abuse. The basic objective is premeditated—to systematically and methodically torture and terrorize children until they are forced to dissociate. The torture is not a consequence of the loss of temper, but the execution of well-planned, well-thought-out rituals often performed by close relatives. The only escape for the children is to dissociate. They will develop a new personality to enable them to endure various forms of abuse. When the episode is over, the core personality is again in control, and the individual is not conscious of what happened.

Dissociation also serves the purposes of the occult because the children have no day-to-day memory of the atrocities. They go through adolescence and early adulthood with no active memory of what is taking place. Oftentimes, they continue in rituals through their teens and early twenties, unaware of their involvement."

-Glenn Leroy Pace, General authority of the Church of Jesus Christ of Latter-day Saints; Glenn Pace Memo Interview of 60 SRA Survivors

It is important to note that the creation of parts (alters) in SRA is not limited to sex trafficking victims. While some victims may have been specifically programmed to sexually service clients, others may have been programmed for other purposes within the cult, such as carrying out rituals, drug trafficking, violence, or performing other tasks. Additionally, not all victims of SRA are diagnosed with DID, and not all people with DID have a history of SRA.

When interacting with, interviewing, or counseling victims of SRA, it is crucial to understand that their alters and programming were designed to protect the cult and its members. Building trust with these individuals requires compassion, kindness, patience, and consistency, and it may take time to establish a rapport that allows them to share their experiences.

It is also important to ensure that victims of SRA have access to trauma-informed counseling that specializes in treating DID, sex trafficking, and ritual abuse. These individuals require a lot of support, and it is essential to work with trained professionals who understand the complexities of their experiences and can provide appropriate care.

To religious or spiritual communities, it is crucial to understand that the alters created in SRA are not demons, and it is harmful to demonize individuals with DID or fractured parts. These individuals require love, forgiveness, and a safe environment to begin the healing process. With compassion and gentleness, it is possible to help these individuals integrate their fractured personalities and find healing from their trauma.

The good news is that deprogramming is possible, and healing can happen through trauma-informed care, inner healing, and safe community. Often, individuals who have experienced SRA Occult trafficking find healing and freedom in faith-based Christian settings, with trained individuals who serve SRA survivors, due to the spiritual nature of their abuse. Addressing the spiritual aspects of their healing journey is necessary for lasting freedom and shouldn't be judged, ignored, or viewed as mental health psychosis.

With compassion, patience, and survivor-informed support, survivors can be set free from these systems of control and fully restored. I have had the honor of seeing many escape and heal from the complexities of SRA trafficking.

RITUAL MARKS, SYMBOLS, AND OCCULT FRAMEWORKS

For many SRA victims, the torture and occult rituals start while in the womb because SRA is often "familial trafficking" due to the significance of generational lines. Satanists include their semen and bodily fluids in baby bottles and start the perverse programming and sexual abuse when the victim is a newborn. For SRA victims who have multiple high-up roles forced on them by the cult... There is a very calculated track of rituals, holidays, and events that takes place over the course of their lives. For some, sexual marriage to their father and Satan happens at age 12.

There is an SRA occult calendar for rituals with victims. Satanists are very methodical, patterned, and legalistic. SRA and occult traffickers use the calendar to do rituals and torture. It tells them what kind of sacrifices to make and who should be involved. SRA survivors generally feel very triggered leading up to ritual dates due to compacted and layered trauma on the same day annually. The victim's birthday is a very traumatic experience as well.

A common ritual includes the Satanist biting a piece of the female victim's clitoris as a way to mark and claim them as their property. Other Satanists know that if a victim has a chunk of their clitoris missing, that victim has already been claimed and they are not allowed to "own" them, only abuse them. This is important for medical professionals to know when conducting a SANE exam and rape kit. If this is identified, then the patient is likely a SRA

Trafficking Victim and is a part of an occult network. Cult members will try to find them, and they may have a tracking device implanted (explained below).

KABALLAH TREE

Many Satanic Ritual Abuse (SRA) Cults, Secret Societies, and Witches use the Kabbalah Tree for rituals and curses on victims. They believe it is a pathway and roadmap to the highest spiritual powers in the universe. The Occult Trafficker "sets out to conquer the universe," thereby requiring entry into the "darkest levels of the mind." To succeed, he or she must become master of everything in the universe—evil as well as good, cruelty as well as mercy, pain as well as pleasure (Cavendish, 1967:3). The more trauma these trafficker occult leaders, witchcraft covens and groups can inflict upon victims by engaging with the points on the Kabbalah Tree, the more powerful they believe that they become. Their beliefs and goals are to intentionally fracture the victim, creating parts/personalities for different roles in the cult that are surrendered to specific demons and geographical territories.

Sex Trafficking Victims of SRA networks may have experienced torture, burns, bruises, tattoos, cuts, and/or scars, illegal surgeries, or restraints in patterns on their bodies. Specifically, on what the cult believes to be spiritual gateways for internal and universal structures in the soul and spirit realm. If patterned marks on the body of a victim are identified, please don't touch the victim in these places.

Codes for hypnosis, curses, brainwashing, and mind control are connected with these areas of the body. They are very triggering to the victim.

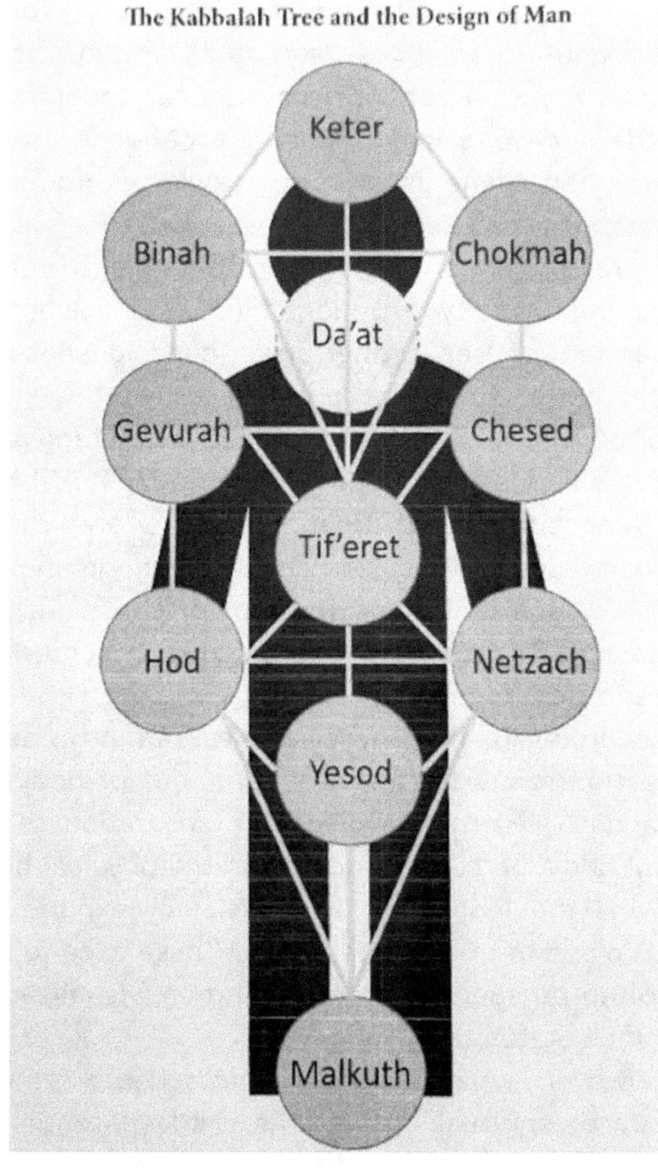

Photo By Dan Duval, Bride Ministries International

ASTRAL PROJECTION

One particularly complex and often misunderstood area of abuse reported by survivors of SRA is astral projection—specifically, non-consensual or forced out-of-body experiences used as a method of control, spiritual violation, or ritual trauma. Understanding the survivor's language and experience around these phenomena is vital in providing grounded, trauma-informed support.

Astral projection, also referred to as an intentional out-of-body experience (OBE), involves the perception of separating one's consciousness or "astral body" from the physical body. It is often described in spiritual, paranormal, or metaphysical contexts and is associated with exploring non-physical dimensions, lucid dreaming, and altered states of awareness. While some view this phenomenon as a form of spiritual empowerment or consciousness expansion, it is also a concept found in occult and esoteric traditions.

According to the Encyclopedia Britannica, astral projection refers to "an intentional out-of-body experience (OBE) that involves the separation of the 'astral body' or 'subtle body' from the physical body, allowing the individual to consciously explore the astral plane or other dimensions." These experiences are often pursued through meditation, visualization, or trance states.

However, what is often overlooked in mainstream or spiritual discussions is the potential for non-consensual or forced forms of this experience, particularly in the context of ritual abuse and trauma-based mind control.

FORCED ASTRAL PROJECTION

Survivors of Satanic Ritual Abuse (SRA) and certain forms of organized trauma frequently describe what I refer to as "forced astral projection," a phenomenon where individuals report being spiritually or energetically pulled from their bodies against their will. These experiences are often described in conjunction with rituals, psychological programming, abuse, or exploitation.

In these accounts, the process is not voluntary and is typically accompanied by extreme trauma, coercion, or threats. Survivors describe being subjected to spiritual assault, ritual violation, psychological torment, or forms of "programming" while in a perceived non-physical state. Some survivors link these experiences to enforced dissociation or altered states created through intense physical and psychological manipulation.

In many cases, these phenomena are described by survivors as involving non-consensual agreements, such as vows, contracts, or permissions given under duress—particularly during childhood abuse or multigenerational rituals. These "agreements" may be coerced, symbolic, or part of programmed belief systems instilled through trauma.

It is critical for service providers, counselors, and investigators to recognize that these narratives—whether understood as literal, symbolic, or trauma-induced memory—are often deeply real to the survivor. These accounts may reflect complex internal experiences rooted in dissociation, spiritual belief systems, and severe trauma conditioning. Regardless of one's personal belief about the metaphysical reality of astral projection, the psychological and emotional impact on the survivor is profound and deserves validation, safety, and skilled, trauma-informed care.

ONGOING RISK AND SPIRITUAL HARASSMENT

Many survivors are stalked or harassed after escape. Cults work to retrieve those who held high roles within their systems, especially if the survivor has information that could expose high-level perpetrators. This stalking may involve physical tracking, cyberstalking, impersonation, spiritual attacks, or even implanted tracking devices. The risk increases around occult calendar dates.

Survivors may also describe spiritual harassment, such as demonic dreams, astral assaults in the spirit realm (explained in the next section), or recurring symbolic contact (like text messages with code words or images to program and trigger trauma memories). These experiences are real and debilitating, and must be taken seriously.

WHY SURVIVORS AREN'T BELIEVED

Sadly, there are still those within the anti-trafficking movement who choose not to believe the testimonies of survivors who have endured satanic ritual abuse (SRA) and programming during their trafficking. This disbelief often stems from a long-standing campaign, known as the 'Satanic Panic,' which was originally orchestrated to discredit and silence the voices of SRA and mind control survivors. This campaign leveraged media and even government reports to portray survivors as suffering from a mental health psychosis rather than acknowledging the reality of their trauma.

Sociologist Michael Salter has written extensively on this issue, noting that:

"Organized abuse is not only a form of violence but also a form of knowledge suppression, where the production of ignorance is a deliberate strategy employed by perpetrators to evade detection and accountability."

— Michael Salter, The Ant epistemology of Organized Abuse

In faith-based settings, this disbelief can be further compounded by theological differences. Some religions or Christian denominations do not believe in the reality of the spiritual realm. This limited perspective makes it difficult for them to comprehend the profound spiritual and psychological impacts of SRA, leading them to dismiss or misunderstand survivors' experiences.

This lack of belief and understanding is not just a theological issue; it has real consequences for survivors seeking healing. When survivors bravely share their stories only to be met with skepticism, dismissal, and a "mental health psychosis," it compounds their trauma and erodes their trust. Such a response is deeply grieving and harmful. If service providers cannot acknowledge the world history, biblical history, and current realities of SRA occult trafficking, they risk causing further damage to those they aim to help.

STATEMENTS SRA SURVIVORS MAY SAY

The following statements are examples of things survivors of SRA trafficking may express. They are provided for awareness and educational purposes only, not for diagnosis. These insights can help service providers, counselors, ministers, and advocates recognize signs of Satanic Ritual Abuse and respond with compassion.

When a survivor shares something that may sound unusual, supernatural, or beyond your personal experience, it is essential to listen without judgment or disbelief. Their reality has been shaped by extreme trauma, manipulation, and programming. Even if what they share challenges your worldview, their experiences are real to them, and their healing depends on being heard, seen, and believed.

1. I vividly remember being subjected to disturbing rituals that involved satanic symbols, chanting, and ceremonies.
2. I was involved with a cult-like group that practiced rituals based on satanic beliefs.

3. Members of a cult abused me physically, psychologically, and spiritually.
4. I was forced to participate in violent and harmful acts as part of satanic rituals.
5. I witnessed others being subjected to rituals, sexual abuse, and violence.
6. I often felt numb, dissociated, or experienced altered states of consciousness during or after the ritual events.
7. I believe that I was manipulated or programmed to forget or repress memories related to the abuse.
8. My trafficking happened at ritual locations.
9. Witchcraft was done to me by my abusers and traffickers.
10. My abusers would often put burns or marks on my body in patterns.
11. I was pulled out of my body and abused in the spirit realm.
12. I have suffered with being rapped by demons.
13. My abusers travel in the spirit realm to me at night.
14. I was forced to endure programming and conditioning. I had to obey, or I was tortured.
15. My father and mother were the first people who sexually abused and sold me.
16. I was forced to endure several types of torture and interrogation.
17. There were occult groups, councils, lodges, or covens involved in controlling me.
18. I was forced to give permission, sign contracts, or be in covenant with people, demons, and places.

19. I was forced out of my body to travel to altars and programming locations at night.
20. The Kabbalah was involved in my abuse.
21. I think I have a device or microchip that they put in me.
22. My traffickers used scriptures and twisted them during rituals, ceremonies, and abuse.
23. My traffickers told me that Satan is god and I was forced to worship him.
24. Some parts of me were given jobs and titles/names by my abusers.
25. My abusers speak in code words to me and text me pictures of symbols, which is very triggering and confusing.

TOUCH, DEVICES, AND ENVIRONMENTAL TRIGGERS

Survivors may have trauma around specific colors, words, music, symbols, and even touch. For example, certain gestures (like shoulder taps) may be associated with rituals. It is important for service providers to be aware of the potential triggers that could re-traumatize these individuals, including how they touch or hug them.

Victims of trafficking and SRA have experienced physical and sexual abuse at the hands of their abusers. This can result in a heightened sensitivity to touch and physical contact, and it may be triggering for them to be touched without their consent. Even seemingly innocent gestures, like patting someone on the shoulder, can bring back memories of past abuse and cause emotional distress.

It is crucial for individuals trying to help to be sensitive to the victim's body language and personal space, and to ask for their permission before touching or hugging them. This is true trauma-informed care that protects felt safety, while honoring and empowering survivor choice. Victims of trafficking and SRA need to feel that they have control over their own bodies and personal space, and that their boundaries are being respected. Asking for permission before touching can also help to establish trust and build a rapport with the victim.

Please don't take it personally if a victim says no to physical contact. This is not a reflection of their own actions, but rather a reflection of the victim's trauma and their need for control over their own body. Instead, continue to offer support and care for the victim in other ways, while respecting their boundaries and choices.

Using the same example: repeatedly patting an SRA survivor on the shoulder, to "encourage" them, may be triggering because it is how a ritual is started and coded with that victim. Remember the Kabbalah Tree points.

DEVICES

In recent years, technological advancements have introduced devices like Neuralink's brain-computer interfaces, which implant microchips into the brain to facilitate direct communication with computers.

While these innovations aim to enhance human capabilities, similar technologies are misused for malicious purposes. Devices have been used within SRA, Trafficking, and government mind-controlled victims for many years.

Inner Ear Devices - Some victims may undergo surgeries to implant devices in the inner ear, enabling traffickers to access the vagal nerve through methods like Morse code tapping or direct speech. This can result in victims displaying behaviors such as finger-tapping patterns during dissociative episodes and switching personality parts.

Subdermal Tracking Implants - Traffickers may implant tracking devices beneath the victim's skin, similar to pet microchips, to monitor their location and prevent escape. These implants facilitate continuous exploitation by allowing abusers to locate and control victims at all times.

REMOVING OCCULT ITEMS AND MARKINGS

SRA victims are often subjected to physical, emotional, and psychological trauma, and the cult's use of cursed jewelry, tattoos, and other ritual items can add to their distress. These items can be powerful reminders of their traumatic experiences and their connection to programming, curses, and the cult.

Removing these items can be a significant step toward healing and finding freedom from the cult's influence. When the survivor is ready, it is important to support them in this process. It must be their choice to get rid of these items, as they may have conflicting emotions about them. It is essential to provide them with a safe and non-judgmental environment to express their feelings and make their own decisions.

The process of removing these items can be liberating for many reasons. It represents the survivor overcoming their fear of the cult members and breaking any agreements or contracts connected with the gifts of jewelry or tattoos. It is also a physical act of taking back control over their body and their life. Removing these items can be a symbolic representation of the survivor's journey toward healing and reclaiming their power.

It is crucial to ensure that the survivor has access to professional support during this process. They may need emotional support, counseling, or medical attention, depending on their individual needs. It is Important to work with trained professionals who have experience working with survivors of complex trauma and ritual abuse.

INVESTIGATION TIP FOR LAW ENFORCEMENT

For Law Enforcement, when doing investigations, know that often the Cult Leaders and Satanists usually have a locked file cabinet with copies of "contracts" that they forced victims to sign during torture and abuse, a forced "agreement." This is how they convince the victims that they have "legal rights" to do whatever they want to them, and that the victim will be criminalized if they ever tell. For the sake of investigations, if found, it would reveal victims' names and crimes against them. These contracts may also reveal lodges or businesses involved in the crimes against the victims.

Though the realities described in this chapter are some of the most disturbing and difficult to comprehend, it's important to remember this: healing is possible. Even for those who have endured the most extreme forms of exploitation and psychological control, recovery can happen. Survivors are not broken beyond repair; they are individuals who carry immense strength, courage, and capacity for restoration. I am an example and proof of that. With consistent, trauma-informed support, safe environments, and the freedom to process their stories on their own terms, survivors can reclaim their identities, rebuild trust, and experience meaningful healing. Every survivor deserves a future that is no longer defined by what was done to them but shaped by the hope of what is still possible.

ADDITIONAL RESOURCES

Out of Shadows documentary: www.intothelight.movie

Resource library: www.SulaLael.com → "Training Resource Library" in the Website Footer → Password: ITMresources

NOTES

CHAPTER 7

SRA TRAFFICKING SURVIVOR AFTERCARE OPTIONS

HONORING SPIRITUAL COMPLEXITY IN SRA OCCULT SURVIVOR AFTERCARE

For some survivors of occult or ritual abuse, the nature of their trauma includes deeply spiritual components that require thoughtful and specialized support. While not every survivor may be ready or interested in addressing these areas, those who are often benefit from care that acknowledges the impact of spiritual programming, ritual experiences, and identity-based fragmentation. Survivors should never be coerced into spiritual care, but when they express interest, they deserve access to safe, trauma-informed environments led by those with lived experience and proper training in this unique area of need.

For those looking for spiritually integrated, survivor-informed support, resources such as the *Take Flight Survivor Community* provide faith-based, peer-led spaces where individuals can explore healing at their own pace. These communities are designed with safety, gentleness, and choice at the core—honoring each survivor's agency while offering hope and support from those who understand. Whether through mentorship, trauma-informed spiritual care, or peer connection, survivors should have access to care that honors the full complexity of their experiences—body, soul, and spirit.

AFTER IDENTIFICATION & BEFORE ESTABLISHING A CARE PLAN
BUILD TRUST WITH SRA SURVIVORS

Before diving into counseling, therapy, or any form of inner healing session, it's crucial to acknowledge the profound trauma SRA survivors have experienced—often at the hands of people who misused roles of authority, including therapists, clergy, or trusted adults. Trust can be difficult to earn. One effective strategy is to begin with a casual, low-pressure meeting that simply allows for connection. This gives the survivor space to observe and gradually become more at ease before engaging in deep or vulnerable work.

For SRA survivors, a common trauma response is the "fawn" reaction—appearing compliant or agreeable as a survival mechanism, even when uncomfortable or internally distressed. This makes it especially important not to misinterpret politeness as readiness. Familiarity, consistency, and patience are key in building genuine trust that lays the foundation for meaningful care.

SETTING THE PACE FOR HEALING

Empowering survivors to determine the pace of their healing is essential. Pushing someone to confront trauma before they are emotionally, mentally, or spiritually ready can increase the risk of re-traumatization, dissociation, or suicidal ideation. Service providers may observe rapid "switching" between parts or protective responses when a survivor is overwhelmed. Before initiating deeper healing work, it's important to first help them establish tools for grounding, emotional regulation, and safety—especially during moments of solitude, such as nighttime, when distress may intensify.

SELECTING THE BEST CARE OPTIONS FOR RITUAL ABUSE SURVIVORS

Trauma-informed care always begins with safety and choice. Clear communication and collaborative decision-making are vital when outlining any care plan. What works for one survivor may not be appropriate for another—particularly when it comes to survivors of ritual abuse.

For example, while EMDR (Eye Movement Desensitization and Reprocessing) is widely used in trauma recovery, it may not be suitable for survivors of SRA unless extensive dissociative screening is completed. The International Society for the Study of Trauma and Dissociation (ISSTD) stresses the importance of assessing for dissociative symptoms, as using standard EMDR on individuals with unrecognized dissociation can result in harm. Some techniques—such as tapping or light bars—may inadvertently mimic ritual programming. Survivors deserve full, unbiased information and the right to decline or delay participation.

The same level of care should extend to other areas of support, including medical visits, counseling intake, or optional group activities. A weekly schedule, open conversations about upcoming events, and permission to ask questions all help foster trust and reduce fear.

HOLISTIC CARE OPTIONS TO CONSIDER FOR SEX TRAFFICKING SURVIVORS OF OCCULT OR SATANIC RITUAL ABUSE (SRA)

Organized by Body, Soul, and Spirit Needs

BODY – COMMON EXPERIENCES

1. Severe sexual and physical trauma, sometimes involving sharp objects, illegal surgeries, or invasive abuse.

2. Body markings, such as patterned burns or cuts, possibly linked to occult rituals.
3. Torture methods resembling military interrogation (e.g., electroshock, restraints, electric collars).
4. Long-term isolation in confined spaces like cages or closets.
5. Implantation of tracking or auditory devices, use of experimental substances.
6. Denial of basic needs like food, hydration, or bathroom access.

BODY – CARE OPTIONS TO CONSIDER (WHEN THE SURVIVOR IS READY):

- Medical exams, including SANE rape kits and wellness checks.
- Imaging (X-ray, MRI) to check for embedded devices.
- Support for restoring healthy sleep and nutrition.
- Trauma-informed support for bathroom use and related bodily functions.

SOUL/MIND & EMOTIONS – COMMON EXPERIENCES

1. Fragmentation of self (e.g., distinct internal parts or personalities), often linked to programmed roles or cult involvement.
2. Psychological programming by handlers or abusers for control or loyalty.

3. Binding covenants, soul ties, or exploitative agreements made under duress.

SOUL – CARE OPTIONS TO CONSIDER (WHEN THE SURVIVOR IS READY):

- Therapy with professionals trained in dissociation and ritual abuse.
- Peer support from lived-experience mentors who can offer hope and solidarity.
- Grounding techniques for managing flashbacks, parts work, and dissociation.
- Addressing trauma-linked agreements through guided therapeutic tools.
- Mind renewal through truth-based reprocessing (secular or faith-based options available depending on survivor choice).
- Encouragement of self-compassion and healing for all parts, including those loyal to the abuser.

Note: Soul/Mind fragmentation is not the same as spiritual possession. Dissociated parts are not demons and should never be treated as such. Mishandling this can result in severe psychological harm.

SPIRITUAL REALM – COMMON EXPERIENCES

1. Experiences described as forced spiritual displacement (e.g., being taken to ritual sites or experiencing astral abuse).
2. Nighttime assaults in dreams or spiritual encounters by abusers.

3. "Spirit rapes" or intrusive experiences described during sleep, often involving terror or programming reinforcement.

SPIRITUAL REALM – CARE OPTIONS (WHEN THE SURVIVOR IS READY):

- Survivors may need space to process the spiritual layers of their trauma. For some, this includes identifying ritual symbolism, confronting spiritual abuse, or disentangling from harmful belief systems.
- Spiritual care—if desired by the survivor—should never be forced. It must be survivor-led, compassionate, and informed by expertise in religious trauma and spiritual abuse recovery.
- Some survivors may seek faith-based healing from leaders or spaces they trust. For those interested, *Take Flight Survivor Community* provides access to peer-led, Christian-informed spiritual support, prayer resources, and tools designed with both trauma and faith in mind. Participation is always voluntary and based on readiness.

FINAL REFLECTION

Ritual abuse trafficking survivors face some of the most complex trauma in the world. Their care must be multifaceted, trauma-informed, and flexible enough to support healing across every area of life—physical, emotional, psychological, and spiritual.

While spiritual needs are deeply personal, many survivors express the need to process what they've experienced on a spiritual level. This may include confronting abusive belief systems, understanding internal conflicts related to faith, or reclaiming their spiritual autonomy. For those who desire it, having access to Christian survivor-informed support can be a powerful part of that journey.

Above all, honoring the survivor's voice and readiness must remain central to every step of care. With informed, non-coercive support systems in place, survivors can move toward freedom, stability, and lasting healing—on their own terms.

NOTES

HOW TO REPORT POTENTIAL TRAFFICKING

Take note of Who? What? How? Where? Why? When? Any details you can remember will be helpful when making a report. What was the potential victim or trafficker wearing? What nationality? What did they look like? How old? Did they have any tattoos, scars, or marks? Vehicle model, make, color? Address?

Anytime someone is under the age of 18 and you suspect sexual abuse, physical abuse or trafficking, you have to report it as a "Mandatory Reporter." You could go to jail if you are aware and did not report it. Anyone under the age of 18 is in the sex industry or providing sexual services to people for the benefit/gain of someone else... That minor, by legal definition, is considered a trafficking victim.

CONTACT

- Rescue America Hotline 833-599-3733
- Law Enforcement (In the county of the suspected trafficking)
- Your State Abuse Hotline
- Human Trafficking Hotline 888-373-7888

***In most cases, the victim's consent is needed in order to arrest the trafficker. A Survivor Leader Advocate is recommended to walk alongside the victim in the reporting and aftercare process.

A NOTE FROM SURVIVOR LEADER, SULA

Dear Reader,

Thank you, from the depths of my heart, for taking the time to journey through this book. Your willingness to engage with such difficult and complex realities is rare and meaningful. It speaks to the compassion, courage, and integrity within you.

This book was not easy to write, and I know it may not have been easy to read. Yet you stayed. You leaned in. You listened. That sets you apart as someone who carries truth with both strength and care.

Whether you are a survivor, a service provider, a loved one, or someone who simply cares—you are part of the solution. Your presence in this work matters.

If you'd like to go deeper, I invite you to explore our survivor-informed training and support resources at **www.TakeFlightSurvivors.org**. You'll find tools, courses, and a community built to strengthen and equip you for this vital work.

With love and heartfelt gratitude,
Sula Lael

ABOUT THE AUTHOR

Sula Lael's journey in the anti-trafficking movement is deeply personal and empowering, stemming from her own formidable experience of overcoming sex trafficking and a painful past. Since 2010, she has devoted herself to raising awareness, training service providers, championing prevention, and assisting fellow survivors of exploitation. With a wealth of experience, she has aided countless victims in escape, healing, and transition to a renewed life.

Serving as a Minister, accomplished author of six books, and a dedicated Sex Trafficking Abolitionist, Sula is a passionate advocate, particularly for survivors grappling with severe mental health diagnoses and those with SRA/occult backgrounds, resulting from the trauma endured in the sex industry.

In 2022, she furthered her commitment to the cause by founding TAKE FLIGHT SURVIVORS, a 501(c)(3) nonprofit organization aimed at supporting and empowering survivors to rebuild and soar to new heights. Sula Lael's unwavering dedication and compassionate approach continue to inspire and bring hope to those she serves, and to the individuals and organizations called to make a difference in the lives of survivors of sex trafficking.

You can read her full story in her book titled, "Fighting for Your Purpose - From Sex Trafficking to Ministry." Available on Amazon.

www.ingramcontent.com/pod-product-compliance
Lightning Source LLC
Chambersburg PA
CBHW070740250726
48662CB00004B/1595